AMAZING ANIMALS OF THE WORLD ③

Volume 9

Spider, Common House — Tuna, Albacore

GROLIER

an imprint of

SCHOLASTIC

Scholastic Library Publishing

www.scholastic.com/librarypublishing

First published 2006 by Grolier, an imprint of Scholastic Library Publishing

For information address the publisher: Grolier, Scholastic Library Publishing
90 Old Sherman Turnpike
Danbury, CT 06816

10 digit: Set ISBN: 0-7172-6179–4; Volume ISBN: 0-7172-6188–3
13 digit: Set ISBN: 978-0-7172-6179–6; Volume ISBN: 978-0-7172-6188–8

Printed and bound in the U.S.A.

Library of Congress Cataloging-in-Publications Data:
Amazing animals of the world 3.
p.cm.
Includes indexes.
Contents: v. 1. Abalone, Black–Butterfly, Giant Swallowtail -- v. 2. Butterfly, Indian Leaf–Dormouse, Garden -- v. 3. Duck, Ferruginous–Glassfish, Indian -- v. 4. Glider, Sugar–Isopod, Freshwater -- v. 5. Jackal, Side-Striped–Margay -- v. 6. Markhor–Peccary, Collared -- v. 7. Pelican, Brown–Salamander, Spotted -- v. 8. Salamander, Two Lined–Spider, Barrel -- v. 9. Spider, Common House–Tuna, Albacore -- v. 10. Tunicate, Light-Bulb–Zebra, Grevy's.
ISBN 0–7172–6179–4 (set : alk. paper) -- ISBN 0–7172–6180–8 (v. 1 : alk. paper) -- ISBN 0–7172–6181–6 (v. 2 : alk. paper) -- ISBN 0-7172-6182–4 (v. 3 : alk. paper) -- ISBN 0-7172-6183–2 (v. 4 : alk. paper) -- ISBN 0-7172-6184–0 (v. 5 : alk. paper) -- ISBN 0-7172-6185–9 (v. 6 : alk. paper) -- ISBN 0-7172-6186–7 (v. 7 : alk. paper) -- ISBN 0-7172-6187–5 (v. 8 : alk. paper) -- ISBN 0-7172-6188–3 (v. 9 : alk. paper) -- ISBN 0-7172-6189–1 (v. 10 : alk.paper)
1. Animals--Juvenile literature. I. Grolier (Firm) II. Title: Amazing animals of the world three.
QL49.A455 2006
590—dc22
                                                                                                    2006010870

About This Set

Amazing Animals of the World 3 brings you pictures of 400 exciting creatures, and important information about how and where they live.

Each page shows just one species, or individual type, of animal. They all fall into seven main categories, or groups, of animals (classes and phylums scientifically) identified on each page with an icon (picture)—amphibians, arthropods, birds, fish, mammals, other invertebrates, and reptiles. Short explanations of what these group names mean, and other terms used commonly in the set, appear on page 4 in the Glossary.

Scientists use all kinds of groupings to help them sort out the types of animals that exist today and once wandered the earth (extinct species). *Kingdoms*, *classes*, *phylums*, *genus*, and *species* are among the key words here that are also explained in the Glossary.

Where animals live is important to know as well. Each of the species in this set lives in a particular place in the world, which you can see outlined on the map on each page. And in those places, the animals tend to favor a particular habitat—an environment the animal finds suitable for life—with food, shelter, and safety from predators that might eat it. There they also find ways to coexist with other animals in the area that might eat somewhat different food, use different homes, and so on.

Each of the main habitats is named on the page and given an icon, or picture, to help you envision it. The habitat names are further defined in the Glossary on page 4.

As well as being part of groups like species, animals fall into other categories that help us understand their lives or behavior. You will find these categories in the Glossary on page 4, where you will learn about carnivores, herbivores, and other types of animals.

And there is more information you might want about an animal—its size, diet, where it lives, and how it carries on its species—the way it creates its young. All these facts and more appear in the data boxes at the top of each page.

Finally, the set is arranged alphabetically by the most common name of the species. That puts most beetles, for example, together in a group so you can compare them easily.

But some animals' names are not so common, and they don't appear near others like them. For instance, the chamois is a kind of goat or antelope. To find animals that are similar—or to locate any species—look in the Index at the end of each book in the set (pages 45–48). It lists all animals by their various names (you will find the Giant South American River Turtle under Turtle, Giant South American River, and also under its other name—Arrau). And you will find all birds, fish, and so on gathered under their broader groupings.

Similarly, smaller like groups appear in the Set Index as well—butterflies include swallowtails and blues, for example.

Table of Contents
Volume 9

Glossary

Amphibians—species usually born from eggs in water or wet places, which change (metamorphose) into land animals. Frogs and salamanders are typical. They breathe through their skin mainly and have no scales.

Arctic and Antarctic—icy, cold, dry areas at the ends of the globe that lack trees but see small plants grown in thawed areas (tundra). Penguins and seals are common inhabitants.

Arthropods—animals with segmented bodies, hard outer skin, and jointed legs, such as spiders and crabs.

Birds—born from eggs, these creatures have wings and often can fly. Eagles, pigeons, and penguins are all birds, though penguins cannot fly through the air.

Carnivores—they are animals that eat other animals. Many species do eat each other sometimes, and a few eat dead animals. Lions kill their prey and eat it, while vultures clean up dead bodies of animals.

Cities, Towns, and Farms—places where people live and have built or used the land and share it with many species. Sometimes these animals live in human homes or just nearby.

Class—part or division of a phylum.

Deserts—dry, often warm areas where animals often are more active on cooler nights or near water sources. Owls, scorpions, and jack rabbits are common in American deserts.

Endangered—some animals in this set are marked as endangered because it is possible they will become extinct soon.

Extinct—these species have died out altogether for whatever reason.

Family—part of an order.

Fish—water animals (aquatic) that typically are born from eggs and breathe through gills. Trout and eels are fish, though whales and dolphins are not (they are mammals).

Forests and Mountains—places where evergreen (coniferous) and leaf-shedding (deciduous) trees are common, or that rise in elevation to make cool, separate habitats. Rain forests are different. (see Rain forests)

Fresh Water—lakes, rivers, and the like carry fresh water (unlike Oceans and Shores, where the water is salty). Fish and birds abound, as do insects, frogs, and mammals.

Genus—part of a family.

Grasslands—habitats with few trees and light rainfall. Grasslands often lie between forests and deserts, and they are home to birds, coyotes, antelope, and snakes, as well as many other kinds of animals.

Herbivores—these animals eat mainly plants. Typically they are hoofed animals (ungulates) that are common on grasslands, such as antelope or deer. Domestic (nonwild) ones are cows and horses.

Hibernators—species that live in harsh areas with very cold winters slow down their functions then and sort of sleep through the hard times.

Invertebrates—animals that lack backbones or internal skeletons. Many, such as insects and shrimp, have hard outer coverings. Clams and worms are also invertebrates.

Kingdom—the largest division of species. Commonly there are understood to be five kingdoms: animals, plants, fungi, protists, and monerans.

Mammals—these creatures usually bear live young and feed them on milk from the mother. A few lay eggs (monotremes like the platypus) or nurse young in a pouch (marsupials like opossums and kangaroos).

Migrators—some species spend different seasons in different places, moving to where more food, warmth, or safety can be found. Birds often do this, sometimes over long distances, but other types of animals also move seasonally, including fish and mammals.

Oceans and Shores—seawater is salty, often deep, and huge. In it live many fish, invertebrates, and even some mammals, such as whales. On the shore, birds and other creatures often gather.

Order—part of a class.

Phylum—part of a kingdom.

Rain forests—here huge trees grow among many other plants helped by the warm, wet environment. Thousands of species of animals also live in these rich habitats.

Reptiles—these species have scales, lungs to breathe, and lay eggs or give birth to live young. Dinosaurs are thought to have been reptiles, while today the class includes turtles, snakes, lizards, and crocodiles.

Scientific name—the genus and species name of a creature in Latin. For instance, Canis lupus is the wolf. Scientific names avoid the confusion possible with common names in any one language or across languages.

Species—a group of the same type of living thing. Part of an order.

Subspecies—a variant but quite similar part of a species.

Territorial—many animals mark out and defend a patch of ground as their home area. Birds and mammals may call quite small or quite large spots their territories.

Vertebrates—animals with backbones and skeletons under their skins

Common House Spider

Tegenaria domestica

Length: ¼ to ½ inch (female);
  ¼ to ⅜ inch (male)
Method of Reproduction: egg
  layer

Diet: flying insects
Home: worldwide
Order: Spiders
Family: Funnel-web spiders

 Cities, Towns,
and Farms

 Arthropods

Almost everyone has seen a common house spider. This arthropod spins its webs in the corners of homes, garages, and other buildings. Like many animals that coexist with human beings, the common house spider is found throughout the world. It has traveled from continent to continent hidden in people's belongings. Next time you find a spider inside your house, look to see if it matches this description.

First look closely at the spider's web. The common house spider usually spins a web in the shape of a tunnel. This tunnel is the spider's home. The web includes a tangle of threads that will trap insects for the spider to eat. If you make a small hole in the web and wait for a day or two, the spider will likely patch the damage. Other kinds of spiders, such as the garden spider, will not repair a damaged web. Instead, they start a new web from scratch. But the house spider is more frugal with its silk and will simply repair its web again and again.

Occasionally you may find a web with two common house spiders on it. Most species of spider would never share their nest. But a female common house spider will allow a male to live on her nest during the egg-laying season. When the female lays her eggs, she encloses them in a ball of silk to protect them from any egg-eating animals that may come along.

Bread Crust Sponge
Halichondria panicea

Diameter of the Colony: 12 inches or more
Height of the Colony: 2 inches
Methods of Reproduction: sexually and asexually

Diet: microscopic organisms
Home: coastal waters of northern Europe
Order: Halichondrids
Family: Ciocalyptids

 Oceans and Shores

Other Invertebrates

© ANDREW J. MARTINEZ / PHOTO RESEARCHERS

Bread crust sponges grow in colonies on rocks and other solid surfaces in coastal waters of northern Europe. They live on the undersides of rocks, beneath seaweed, and in other protected places where they will not be exposed to sun when the tide goes out. They never move around; they remain in one spot their entire lives.

The colonies are usually greenish in color, but they may be yellowish or orange. Sometimes bread-crust-sponge colonies of different colors grow side by side. This animal's name comes from the texture of dried pieces of sponge: they look and feel like bread crusts. But they do not smell like bread. Like many sponges, the bread crust sponge has a strong, unpleasant odor.

A close look at the bread-crust-sponge colony reveals an interesting feature: the surface is evenly dotted with what look like tiny volcanoes. Each animal in the colony has one of these holes at its top end. Water enters the individual sponge animal through pores in its sides. Cells in the animal remove food and oxygen. Then the water is forced out through the "volcano." When the sponge animal senses harmful substances in its environment, it can close its openings. This prevents polluted water from flowing through the sponge. This works for only a short time, however. Soon the sponge must have food and oxygen, or it will die.

Roseate Spoonbill
Ajaja ajaja

Length: 32 inches
Number of Eggs: usually 3
Home: from Florida and the Gulf states to Argentina and Chile

Diet: frogs, crustaceans, insects, and small fish
Order: Storks and their relatives
Family: Spoonbills and ibises

 Fresh Water

 Birds

© DARRELL GULIN / CORBIS

The roseate spoonbill stands knee-deep in a marsh, dipping its partly open beak in the water and swishing it from side to side. The spoonbill is hunting by touch. Its spatula-shaped bill automatically snaps shut as soon as it touches a wriggling animal suitable for a snack. As it hunts, the roseate spoonbill grunts and croaks as if muttering to itself.

During courtship a pair of roseate spoonbills communicate their excitement and affection by clapping their bills together. The male then presents his chosen female with sticks, as if they were precious gifts. In a similar manner, the male continues to bring twigs to his mate as she weaves their platform nest. She builds this sturdy nest above the water, either in branches or among the propped-up roots of a mangrove tree.

Roseate spoonbills are social birds that usually build their nests close together. Spoonbills also migrate as flocks, flying in a "V" formation with their long necks outstretched. These birds are strong fliers that often glide between strokes of their large, powerful wings.

The world's population of roseate spoonbills was nearly wiped out around the turn of the century. The birds were killed for their beautiful feathers, which were made into ladies' fans. Since the 1940s, however, the roseate spoonbill has been expanding its range in North America.

7

Opalescent Squid
Loligo opalescens

Length of the Body: up to 8 inches (not including tentacles)
Width of the Body: about 1¾ inches
Home: Pacific Ocean

Diet: fish, crustaceans, and mollusks
Method of Reproduction: egg layer
Order: Squids
Family: Common squids

  Oceans and Shores

Other Invertebrates

© MARILYN KAZMERS / PETER ARNOLD, INC.

The creature known as the opalescent squid is most familiar as the food "calamari." In North America, this is the squid commonly sold chopped and frozen in grocery stores and in fish markets. It is caught off the west coast of Canada and the United States during its breeding season. As the squid enters shallow water to spawn, it is scooped up in huge nets by commercial fishing boats. Opalescent squid are also eaten by many coastal fish and marine mammals.

This medium-size squid is cylindrical in shape, with a body that comes to a rounded point at the rear. Its semitransparent skin is mottled with flecks of gold, brown, and red. But the squid can rapidly change color when excited. Like all squid the opalescent has 10 arms, or tentacles. One pair of arms is longer than the rest, measuring about two-thirds the length of the squid's body, with many small suckers. The squid uses its long arms for seizing and grappling with prey.

Like all squid the opalescent moves by jet propulsion. That is, it sucks water into its body cavity and then forces it out through a flexible tube in a strong jet stream. The stream propels the squid's body backward. At the rear of the body are two triangular fins, with which it steers and brakes. Opalescent squid remain in coastal waters year-round. They can be found at all depths, from the surface to the ocean bottom.

8

Cape Bristled Ground Squirrel
Xerus inauris

Length of the Body: about 12 inches
Length of the Tail: about 11 inches
Diet: mainly leaves, seeds, fruits, and roots

Weight: 5 to 10 pounds
Number of Young: usually 2
Home: western South Africa
Order: Rodents
Family: Squirrels

 Deserts

 Mammals

Bristled ground squirrels are named for their sparse coat of stiff, prickly fur, which is quite unlike the soft, thick fur of other squirrels. The Cape bristled ground squirrel is one of six species in this group. Its pale coat is reddish to grayish brown—colored to match the barren ground on which it lives. Adding to the camouflage is a light coating of dust that seems forever stuck to the fur. The species can be further distinguished by its unusual flattened tail. All bristled ground squirrels have small ears, but the ears of the Cape species are almost invisible. In fact, its Latin name, *inauris*, means earless.

The Cape squirrel lives in the deserts and barren grasslands of western South Africa. It is the most familiar of the bristled squirrels because it also inhabits populated areas. The squirrel is most active during the day, when it frequently "bathes," or dusts itself in loose, dry soil. When frightened, it flees into a ground burrow or rock crevice.

Like other bristled ground squirrels, the Cape species is social and gathers in colonies to feed and play. The members take turns eating and keeping watch for danger. Although the squirrel is primarily a vegetarian, it occasionally steals eggs and chicks from nests, and catches insects and lizards. In turn, it is hunted by birds of prey, large snakes, dogs, and cats.

Eurasian Red Squirrel
Sciurus vulgaris

Length of the Body: 6 to 8½ inches
Length of the Tail: 6 to 8 inches
Weight: 7½ to 14½ ounces

Diet: mainly seeds and berries
Number of Young: 3 to 5
Home: Eurasia
Order: Rodents
Family: Squirrels

 Forests and Mountains

 Mammals

© NIALL BENVIE / CORBIS

The Eurasian red squirrel starts eating as soon as it wakes up in the morning. The squirrel gobbles down acorns, seeds, nuts, and berries. It strips bark and mushrooms from the sides of trees and nips off buds from tender young branches. It eats insects and slugs as well. Red squirrels are hungriest in springtime, when they eat as much as half their own body weight in food each day. In summer and fall, they eat somewhat less. And in winter, they must survive on much less. Fortunately, red squirrels know instinctively that they must hoard food for the lean winter season. In fall, they hide acorns and seeds in tree holes and crevices, and bury many rations in the ground.

Eurasian red squirrels make many nests. Most are round tangles of twigs and leaves built at the top of tall trees. These squirrels also stuff grass, leaves, and moss inside tree holes for "indoor" beds. In spring and summer, the nest is used for a midday nap, as well as for nighttime sleeping. In the winter, when food is difficult to find, the red squirrel has little time for napping.

The Eurasian red squirrel spends most of its life high in the trees. When it jumps, the squirrel holds its fluffy tail behind its body for balance. The red squirrel also uses its tail to "talk" with other squirrels. When angry or alarmed, it pumps its tail up and down violently. Red squirrels communicate through chatters and squeaks as well.

Starfish
Asterina gibbosa

Length: 2½ inches
Weight: 4 to 5 ounces
Diet: sponges and small marine animals
Number of Eggs: 2 million to 100 million

Home: Atlantic Ocean from England to the Mediterranean Sea
Order: Small-spined starfishes
Family: Pentagonal-shaped starfishes

 Oceans and Shores

 Other Invertebrates

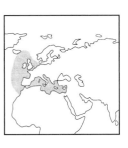

© SUE DALY / NATURE PICTURE LIBRARY

This species of starfish is never born a female, and it never dies of old age as a male. During the first portion of its life, *Asterina gibbosa* reproduces like a male. That is, the young starfish produces sperm. It joins with other young males and gathers around an older female to fertilize her eggs. As the starfish matures, it begins to produce eggs of its own. For a short time, it will produce both eggs and sperm. It will be both male and female! Eventually the "he-now-a-she" produces only eggs and relies on younger starfish to fertilize them.

Though it appears to have no front or back, starfish do have a type of head and tail. Their "head" end contains most of their sensory organs. Starfish tend to move so that this highly sensitive part of their body is facing forward. However, the starfish can move in any direction it likes, since all of its arms are more or less the same size and shape.

The starfish creeps along on hundreds of tiny tube feet that cover the bottom of its arms. Each tube foot ends in a little suction cup. These suction disks are strong enough to keep a starfish stuck firmly to a rock, despite the pulling and pounding of the ocean waves. In fact, if you were to yank a starfish from its perch, many of its feet would tear from the body and remain glued to the rock. Fortunately for the starfish, it can regrow body parts—even an entire arm.

Steinbok
Raphicerus campestris

Length: 2⅓ to 3 feet
Height at the Shoulder: 1½ to 2 feet
Diet: leaves, grasses, and herbs

Weight: 22 to 35 pounds
Number of Young: 1
Home: Africa
Order: Even-toed mammals
Family: Bovines

 Grasslands

© ANTHONY BANNISTER / GALLO IMAGES / CORBIS

Mammals

The steinbok is a dwarf antelope about the size of a German shepherd dog. Its slender neck and long legs give it a delicate, almost fragile appearance. Because its head is small, its broad, erect ears look huge in comparison. The steinbok's tail is a mere stump. Most of these antelope are rusty red or silvery gray. Each adult has a distinctive V-shaped mark across the muzzle.

This antelope was named by early Boer settlers who came to Africa from Europe. The Boers often named African animals after similar European ones, and *steenbok* was the Dutch name for the ibex, a wild goat of the Alps. In reality the African steinbok and the European ibex have little resemblance.

The steinbok lives on the flat savannas of eastern and southern Africa. It is most abundant in areas with tall grasses, which provide limitless hiding places. When frightened, the animal sprints away a short distance and lies down flat in the grass, appearing to vanish from view. It also hides in aardvark burrows.

Usually living alone, each adult establishes a territory and defends it from intruders. Only during the breeding season do steinboks tolerate others of their kind—and then only for mating. After a six-month pregnancy, the female gives birth to a two-pound baby. The youngster stays with its mother for up to four months.

Sterlet
Acipenser ruthenus

Length: up to 40 inches
Diet: snails, insects, and worms
Method of Reproduction: egg layer

Home: Europe and Asia
Order: Sturgeons and paddlefishes
Family: Sturgeons

Fresh Water

Fish

The sterlet is a small sturgeon, much sought for its flavorful meat and eggs, which are made into gourmet caviar. Unfortunately, its legendary good taste has caused the sterlet to be overfished for centuries. More recently the fish has suffered from the pollution of the Danube and Volga rivers, as well as the Caspian Sea. To save this beloved fish, conservationists are trying to clean up Europe's waterways. In addition, several countries have passed laws limiting the size and number of sterlets that can be caught each year. In Germany and Austria, new artificial lakes have been built and stocked with farm-raised sterlets.

The fish is easily recognized by its long, tubular mouth. The sterlet snuffles along the bottoms of lakes and rivers, sucking up food like a vacuum cleaner. Four long, fleshy whiskers dangle from the creature's long snout. These are called "barbels," and the sterlet uses them to feel and taste its food.

Although humans have caught sterlets for hundreds of years, we still know little about their life cycle. Some migrate in the spring to special spawning grounds. In May, small schools swim upstream to gravelly and stony areas. Their journey is difficult, because the rivers are swollen with rushing water from melting snow and ice. The female sterlet lays masses of small gray eggs that stick to the gravel and rocks. Between 4 and 6 inches long when they hatch, the young look like small black tadpoles.

Three-Spined Stickleback
Gasterosteus aculeatus

Diet: small crustaceans, insects, and eggs of other fish
Number of Young: several hundred

Home: Northern Hemisphere
Length: 2 to 4 inches
Order: Tube-mouthed fishes
Family: Sticklebacks

 Fresh Water

 Fish

© WINIFRED WISNIEWSKI / FRANK LANE PICTURE AGENCY / CORBIS

The three-spined stickleback can never, ever sit still. Even when it's not going anywhere, this fish is a whir of motion—its tail and fins vibrating like a hummingbird's wings. Always ready for action, it will pick a fight with a fish three times its own size. Luckily, nature equipped this little creature with armor: two large spines and one small one on its back, as well as many bony shields.

In his courtship the male three-spined stickleback is gallant and energetic. He builds a nest of aquatic plants, which he sticks together with a glue secreted from his kidneys. The male is then ready for a mate. At first the female will be attracted by the male's bright-red throat. Then he will lure her closer with a zigzag dance, chasing and

nipping her until she enters his nest. But as soon as the female lays her eggs, the male chases her away. The stickleback father remains, protecting the nest and carefully fanning the water over the eggs. He continues to care for the young after they are born. If they try to leave the nest before their time, he scoops them up in his mouth and spits them back.

As a whole, this species is quite common. But one subspecies—the unarmored three-spined stickleback—is close to extinction. This subspecies is the center of much controversy in California, where the last few of these fish remain. Their habitat is threatened by developers who want to fill in the water and build houses.

Common European Stonefly
Perla marginata

Length: ⅜ to 1⅝ inches
Wingspan: ⅞ to 2⅜ inches
Diet: microscopic algae and plankton animals
Number of Eggs: up to 1,000

Home: Europe and the Middle East
Order: Stoneflies
Family: Common stoneflies

 Fresh Water

 Arthropods

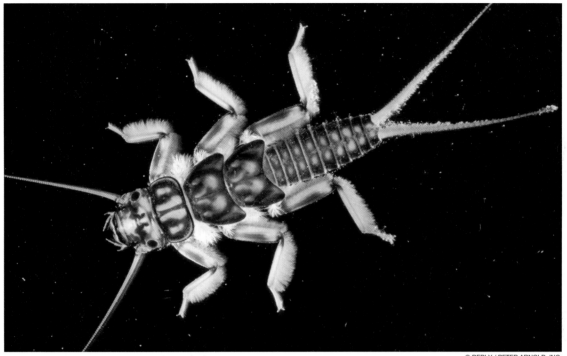

Adult stoneflies are delicate, thin-winged insects, yellow or brown in color. They are poor fliers and spend most of their time sitting on stones, rocks, or conifer trees along rivers or streams. The winged adults live for only two or three weeks in late spring and summer. During this time, they never eat. (Some closely related stoneflies in California feed on fruit trees, causing considerable damage.)

After mating, the female skims over the water surface, dipping her abdomen into the water while depositing her eggs. The sticky eggs cling to underwater rocks, gravel, and plants. The eggs hatch into tiny larvae that have huge appetites for thick green algae and microscopic plankton animals. The larvae breathe through tiny gills located on their legs, belly, and other body parts. Immature stoneflies mature into winged adults in one to three years. During this time, they change body shape several times and molt, or replace their old skin with new skin, over 20 times.

The immature, aquatic stoneflies are an important food source for many popular freshwater fish. People often collect the larvae as food for fish in their home aquariums. But collecting these tiny creatures is a challenging job. One person must roll rocks and gravel upstream to loosen the insects, while a second person holds a net downstream to catch them.

Painted Stork
Mycteria leucocephala

Length: about 40 inches
Weight: about 7 pounds
Diet: fish, frogs, and marine invertebrates
Number of Eggs: 3 to 5

Home: India, China, Burma, Thailand, Cambodia, and Vietnam
Order: Stilt-legged birds
Family: Storks

  Fresh Water

Birds

© BRIAN A. VIKANDER / CORBIS

The painted stork lives in the warm lakes, marshes, and paddy fields of Southeast Asia. Its species name, *leucocephala*, means "white-headed." But the stork is better known for its many colors. The outside of its wings look as if they have been lightly brushed with pink paint. The bird's bill is bright yellow, and its feet are often red. The painted stork is most colorful during the breeding season, when its naked face turns bright red! Young painted storks are not as colorful as their parents. During their first year or two, the immature birds are a dull brown. This helps the inexperienced young hide from their many enemies.

Like others in the stork family, painted storks mate for life. The couple reinforce their lifelong bond with a special greeting dance. They perform it each time one or the other returns to the nest. In this ceremony, the painted storks bob their heads and necks up and down as they hiss and scream with open bills. To complete the greeting, each bird snaps its bill three or four times.

Painted storks build enormous twig nests on top of large branches. Typically the nest is located directly over a marsh or shallow lake. These colorful birds hunt for fish and other aquatic creatures by swishing their long, downward-curving bill through the water. When it touches something alive, the bill snaps shut automatically with amazing speed.

Saddle-Bill Stork
Ephippiorhynchus senegalensis

Length: 5 feet
Wingspan: 6½ feet
Diet: fish and small vertebrates; insects, some rotting meat

Number of Eggs: 1 to 3
Home: Africa south of the Sahara
Order: Stilt-legged birds
Family: Storks

 Fresh Water

 Birds

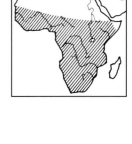

© ML SINIBALDI / CORBIS

Saddle-bill storks are found in Africa south of the Sahara Desert. They are not very sociable and live alone or in pairs. Saddle bills, like common mute swans, can't make sounds. When they want to be noticed at mating time, they click their beaks. Saddle bills are often found near lakeshores and ponds, and on the banks of large rivers. Their legs are long and black with red "patches" on the knees. They move slowly while they catch and eat fish, lizards, and small animals. To eat a fish or a frog, the stork grabs the animal with its beak. The bird then shakes its head until the prey slides to the back of its beak and is swallowed. It can catch grasshoppers and other insects in midair.

The saddle bill has a remarkable beak. It is very long and curves up a little. The beak is bright red with a large ring of black near the face. There is a bright yellow spot over the top part of the beak that makes it look as though the bird is wearing a cap.

It builds a nest made of branches, grass, and all sorts of odds and ends. The female usually lays one egg, which she sits on at night and the male sits on during the day. The young saddle bill hatches from its egg after about one month. The baby stays with the adults for awhile after leaving the nest, but then the family separates. The saddle-bill stork has large black-and-white wings and is a very powerful flier. It may soar for hours, as most storks do.

Water Strider
Gerris remigis

Diet: small aquatic and land insects
Method of Reproduction: egg layer

Length of Body: about ½ inch
Home: North America
Order: Bugs
Family: Water striders

  Fresh Water

Arthropods

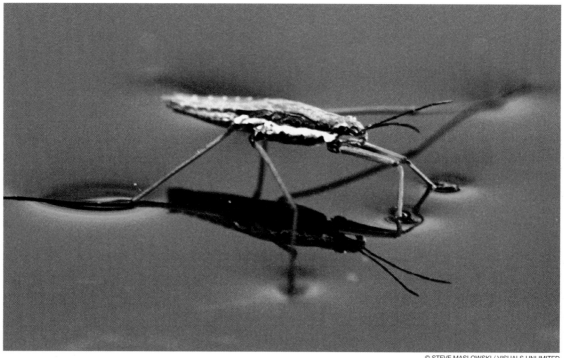

Look closely at a quiet pond or stream on a warm summer day, and you are likely to see tiny creatures darting about on the surface. These long, slender insects with dark brown bodies are water striders. They spend almost their entire lives on the thin surface film of water. They occasionally jump into the air, but neither on takeoff nor when landing do they break through the surface film. Their front legs are short and used to catch and hold prey. The middle and hind legs are long and covered with thin hairs that are water-repellent. The hairs trap tiny air bubbles that help keep the insects afloat. The water strider rows across the surface using its middle legs as oars; the hind legs are used to steer.

Water striders feed mainly on aquatic insects that come to the surface and on dead flies and other insects that fall into the water. They also jump into the air to capture insects.

During courtship, male and female water striders communicate by making ripples in the surface film. After mating, the female cements her eggs onto a plant or other floating object just below the surface. The eggs hatch into young, or nymphs, that look very much like the adults. The nymphs are very active, jumping frequently on the surface. They mature in about five weeks.

Cape Sugarbird
Promerops cafer

Length: up to 17½ inches (male); up to 11½ inches (female)
Diet: mainly nectar; also insects and spiders

Number of Eggs: 2
Home: South Africa
Order: Perching birds
Family: Honey eaters

 Forests and Mountains

 Birds

© PETER JOHNSON / CORBIS

The male cape sugarbird seems to know how unique and lovely he looks. With strikingly long tail feathers and a long, curved bill, he perches on top of bushes, calling and singing. When other males enter his territory, he quickly flies up to chase them away. The female looks like the male, but her tail is much shorter.

The sugarbird lives on mountain slopes covered with protea bushes. These bushes are very important to the bird because they provide food and nesting sites. The sugarbird uses its long bill and brushy tongue to sip nectar from protea flowers. The bird enjoys a fine meal, but it also helps the protea. Pollen from the flower sticks to the sugarbird's bill and feathers. The bird carries the pollen to other protea flowers. This process of pollination ensures that the protea flowers will make seeds.

Cape sugarbirds mate during the South African winter, the time of year when proteas bloom. During courtship the male dances in the air over the nesting site. He claps his wings together, twists and turns his long tail feathers, and performs other acrobatic feats to impress the female. The female builds a cup-shaped nest, usually in a protea bush. The nest, which takes about a week to build, is made of twigs, grasses, and other plant matter, and lined with the soft down of the protea flower. As the female incubates the eggs, her mate defends the surrounding area. Both parents care for the chicks.

Tree Swallow
Tachycineta bicolor

Length: 5 to 6 inches
Wingspan: 12 to 13 inches
Weight: about ½ ounce
Diet: insects, spiders, seeds, and berries

Number of Eggs: 4 to 6
Home: North America and Central America
Order: Perching Birds
Family: Swallows

 Fresh Water

 Birds

© TIM ZUROWSKI / CORBIS

The tree swallow is a small songbird that is well adapted to life in the air. A slender bird with long, pointed wings, it can be found near marshes, ponds, wet meadows, and other wetlands. There it flies back and forth until its sharp eyes spot prey. When a tasty morsel is in sight, the swallow dives, snatching flies, bees, and other insects out of the air. It also lands on the ground to feed on insects, seeds, and berries.

Tree swallows migrate with the seasons, traveling by day in large flocks. They spend the summer months in northern temperate parts of Canada and the United States. As cold weather approaches, they fly south to winter in the southern United States and south into Central America.

Tree swallows fly north early in the year. They may arrive at their summer home while snow still covers the ground. But their arrival announces that spring will soon be here—which is why swallows are called "harbingers of spring."

The male tree swallow courts a female in the air. To attract her, he sings and makes all sorts of acrobatic circles, dives, and other movements. Tree swallows make their nests in tree holes, bird boxes, and cavities under the roofs of barns and houses. The female tree swallow builds the nest from dried grass, then lines it with soft chicken feathers.

Chimney Swift
Chaetura pelagica

Length: 4½ to 5½ inches
Wingspan: about 12½ inches
Weight: about 1 ounce
Diet: insects and spiders
Home: *Summer:* Canada and
the United States

Winter: South America
Number of Eggs: 2 to 7
Order: Swifts and
hummingbirds
Family: Swifts

Cities, Towns, and Farms

☐ Summer
■ Winter

Birds

© STEVE MASLOWSKI / PHOTO RESEARCHERS

The chimney swift gets its name from its favorite nocturnal pastime: roosting in chimneys. During the day chimney swifts fly about much like other birds—looking for food, water, and the perfect mate. Come nightfall, though, dozens of swifts gather at a chimney and circle around. Gradually the flock forms a funnel shape. Slowly, the flock—or "funnel"—descends, bird by bird, until all the birds are in the chimney. They roost close together to keep warm, using the strong claws on their feet to hold on to the vertical surface.

The chimney swift has a short, streamlined body. Although its legs are small and weak, its wing muscles are highly developed. Thus, it is not surprising that the

chimney swift spends much of its time in the air. The chimney swift is a speedy flier. In fact, the swift family of birds are faster fliers than any other small bird. Even their name means fast!

Chimney swifts may also use chimneys to hold their nests, though they often find homes elsewhere, as in barns and hollow trees. The nest is made of twigs. While in flight, the swift uses its feet to break twigs off trees and bushes. At the nest site, the chimney swift arranges the twigs to form a shallow cup. It uses its sticky saliva to glue the twigs together. The parents take turns sitting on the eggs and caring for the babies. Chimney swifts often return to the same nesting place year after year.

21

Eurasian Swift
Apus apus

Length: about 5½ inches
Weight: about 1⅓ ounces
Diet: insects
Home: *Summer:* Eurasia and
northern Africa

Winter: tropical Africa
Number of Eggs: usually 3
Order: Swifts
Family: Swifts

 Cities, Towns,
and Farms

Summer Winter

 Birds

© HANS REINHARD / BRUCE COLEMAN INC.

The only time you are likely to see a Eurasian swift at rest is while it is warming its eggs. When away from the nest, swifts are almost always in flight. They eat, drink, collect grass, and even mate while flying.

Since they seldom walk on the ground or perch in trees, swifts have tiny legs and feet. However, they have strong claws for clinging to vertical walls and cliffs. Like swallows and martins, swifts are equipped with narrow, pointed wings and a forked tail. The Eurasian swift's wings are particularly long and well developed. Its tiny beak opens very wide, enabling the bird to catch insects in the air.

In mid-May, Eurasian swifts breed and choose their nesting sites. Together the mated pair bring grass and feathers to a rock crevice or the eave of a building. Using their sticky saliva as glue, the birds secure the nesting material into place. The female lays her three eggs at intervals of two or three days. After a two- to three-week incubation, the eggs hatch in the same order in which they were laid.

The chicks are fed by both parents, which occasionally disappear for several days at a time. When they do, their chicks get very skinny and stop growing. The young may even lie motionless and appear dead. But they are only in a deep resting state, from which they will recover when the parents arrive with fresh food.

Swordfish
Xiphias gladius

Length: 7 to 10 feet
Weight: 120 to 250 pounds
Diet: fish
Method of Reproduction: egg layer

Home: tropical and temperate oceans and seas
Order: Perchlike fish
Family: Swordfish

 Oceans and Shores

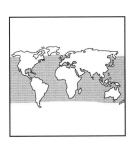

 Fish

© NORBERT WU / PETER ARNOLD, INC.

The "sword" of the swordfish is actually a stretched-out structure that includes the animal's jaw and snout. It can grow to one-third of the fish's total length. The swordfish uses this weapon to stab at schools of fish, stunning and even piercing some of the prey. The swordfish puts up quite a fight when it is attacking or being attacked. Broken pieces of "sword" have been found in sharks, whales, and even in the sides of boats.

Swordfish swim to the warm waters of the Sargasso Sea and, less often, the Mediterranean Sea to spawn. There they lay tiny eggs that float along the surface. Eventually the eggs hatch into larvae with spines and scales. The scales disappear by adulthood. The fully grown swordfish has a white belly, gray-blue sides, and a black-blue back. Swordfish can swim very quickly. They usually go no deeper than 10 feet underwater, although they have been caught at depths as low as 1,200 feet, where they feed on luminous sardines. Only the adults venture from the tropics to the cooler waters to the north.

Swordfish meat is a very popular seafood. Most swordfish are caught using long fishing lines; some are harpooned at the surface. The largest swordfish taken on a hook and line was a 15-foot specimen caught off the coast of Chile. The giant fish weighed over 1,100 pounds.

Tench
Tinca tinca

Length: up to 33 inches
Weight: up to 15 pounds
Diet: insect larvae, small crustaceans, and mollusks
Method of Reproduction: egg layer

Home: Europe and western Asia; introduced elsewhere
Order: Minnows, suckers, and loaches
Family: Minnows

 Fresh Water

Fish

© GERARD LACZ / PETER ARNOLD INC.

Few freshwater fish are as slimy as the tench. Its skin gives off enormous amounts of mucus, making the creature slippery and difficult to hold. It has a thick, heavy body and head, but very small scales. Considering its outward appearance, the meat of the tench is surprisingly tender and tasty. Perch and pike prey on this fish, as do humans, who catch tench with nets or with hooks and lines. Some people even keep young tench in home aquariums.

People also call this creature the "doctor fish," based on the belief that the tench's slime can help heal wounds on other fish. They thought (incorrectly) that the tench encouraged injured fish to rub their wounds on the slime.

The tench has a green or brown back, gray fins, and a pale belly. It does not have teeth in its jaws. Instead, its food is ground by rows of teeth on bones near its gills.

The tench lives among water plants in marshes, quiet ponds, and slow-moving rivers with muddy bottoms. It spends most of the time poking in the mud looking for mollusks and other prey. In winter, tench that live in cold places become inactive. They may even bury themselves in the bottom until warm weather returns. Tench lay their eggs in spring and early summer. The tiny green eggs stick to water plants until they hatch.

Tailless Tenrec
Tenrec ecaudatus

Length: 10 to 16 inches
Diet: mainly worms, grubs, grasshoppers, and other small animals
Number of Young: usually 12 to 15

Weight: 3 to 5 pounds
Home: Madagascar, Comoros, and nearby islands
Order: Insectivores
Family: Tenrecs

 Grasslands

 Mammals

© FRANS LANTING / MINDEN PICTURES

The tailless tenrec is the largest of the tenrecs, a group of insect-eating mammals found primarily on the island of Madagascar. Despite its name, this species does have a short tail, although it is hidden beneath thick fur. The tenrec is covered with spiny hairs that protect the animal from natural predators. However, spines are no defense against human hunters. The people of Madagascar hunt this meaty tenrec and cook it into a curried stew. The natives have also cut down or burned much of the animal's natural habitat.

Still, the tailless tenrec continues to thrive in large numbers. The success of this species is due in large part to its remarkable fertility. A single female can produce up to 32 young a year. Another key to the tenrec's survival is its ability to hibernate through times of drought and scarce food. During Madagascar's dry season, the tenrec disappears into its burrow and sleeps for several months. As the creature hibernates, its body temperature lowers, and its breathing and heart rate slow. An "inner clock" awakens the animal when the spring rains arrive.

Soon after they awaken from hibernation, tailless tenrecs mate. About two months later, the female produces her large litter. The blind, naked newborns are about three inches long and weigh less than an ounce. They become independent when they are seven weeks old.

Diamondback Terrapin
Malaclemys terrapin

Length: 4 to 10 inches
Method of Reproduction: egg layer
Home: eastern and Gulf coasts of the United States

Diet: snails, clams, and worms
Order: Turtles and tortoises
Family: Box turtles and water turtles

 Oceans and Shores

 Reptiles

© DAVID A. NORTHCOTT / CORBIS

Terrapins are North American turtles famous for their tasty meat. The diamondback was considered such a delicacy that it was greatly overhunted in the early 1900s. As a result, its current population is a small fraction of what it was 100 years ago. Recently the diamondback has suffered from the loss of its habitat. Most of the coastal marshes the turtle once inhabited have been filled by land developers. Fortunately, some states now have laws that protect remaining wetlands.

The diamondback is named for its dramatically sculptured top shell, or carapace. The horny plates, or scutes, on the carapace are covered with deep, diamond-shaped growth rings. The skin on the turtle's head, neck, and legs is gray to pink and dotted with many black spots or blotches. There are seven subspecies of diamondback turtle, each recognized by differences in coloring and spot pattern.

While the majority of turtles are vegetarians, diamondbacks prefer meat. They often eat mollusks, worms, and snails on the muddy surfaces of exposed tidal flats. Diamondbacks also search for food in saltwater marshes and in the lagoons that form behind sand dunes. In April and May, mated females dig 4- to 8-inch-deep nesting holes in the sand. Each female deposits a clutch of pink, leathery eggs and buries them in sand.

Black Tetra
Gymnocorymbus ternetzi

Length: up to 3 inches
Diet: insects, small aquatic animals, and plants
Method of Reproduction: egg layer

Home: South America
Order: Carps and their relatives
Family: Characins

 Fresh Water

 Fish

© JANE BURTON / BRUCE COLEMAN INC.

The black tetra is the most familiar fish in its family thanks to its popularity with home aquarium owners. But its name is misleading, because only the young fish are truly black. Black tetras lighten as they grow older, and mature males even develop white spots on their gray tail. The female tends to be larger than her mate and is usually quite plump. Both sexes have two distinct dark bars on each side of their body. Their long, sweeping fins give them an air of grace and elegance.

In the wild, black tetras live in small streams and bogs in the tropical heartland of South America. In captivity, they must be kept in a very warm aquarium. They thrive in water that is between 70 and 90 degrees

Fahrenheit, and will breed only when temperatures are between 80 and 82 degrees. These fish should always be kept with several others of their kind because in nature, black tetras are always found in large groups. When young, they swim in schools that move and turn with dramatic precision. Older tetras live in smaller groups.

Whether in an aquarium or in a jungle stream, black tetras breed in the early-morning sun. As the couple spawns, the female drops her eggs onto the pebbles at the bottom of the tank or stream. In captivity the parents must be quickly removed after spawning, or they will eat their own eggs.

Cardinal Tetra
Cheirodon axelrodi

Length: up to 1½ inches
Diet: small fish, larvae, and invertebrates
Home: Río Negro area of South America

Number of Eggs: 60 to 130
Order: Carps and their relatives
Family: Characins

 Fresh Water

 Fish

© JANE BURTON / BRUCE COLEMAN INC.

The cardinal tetra is one of the most colorful creatures of its kind ever discovered. Shortly after it was found and described in 1956, this species was brought to the United States by aquarium enthusiasts amid great sensation in the pet-fish trade. Today the exotic cardinal tetra is one of the most popular freshwater aquarium fish.

In nature, cardinal tetras live in forest pools alongside the Río Negro, a large river in tropical South America. In the wild, they survive no longer than one year because their habitat contains so little food that most simply starve after they mate and spawn. But in captivity, cardinal tetras live long enough to spawn several times.

The female tetra lays clear, smooth eggs that she places on the leaves and stems of underwater plants. The male fertilizes the eggs as they emerge from the female's body. In an aquarium the male and female must be removed immediately after spawning. Otherwise they may eat some eggs. Also, the tank must be darkened to allow the eggs to mature and hatch. Twenty-two to 26 hours after the eggs are laid, the newborn, called fry, emerge. At first they stay hidden among the plants. But on the fifth day, they begin to swim freely. The male tetras are smaller and slimmer than their sisters. They can also be recognized by the tiny, hooklike structures on their anal fin (the belly fin nearest the tail).

Song Thrush
Turdus philomelos

Length: 9 inches
Diet: insects and their larvae, worms, snails, and fruits
Number of Eggs: usually 4

Home: Europe and Asia
Order: Perching birds
Family: Thrushes

 Cities, Towns, and Farms

 Birds

© ERIC AND DAVID HOSKING / CORBIS

The song thrush is a small brown bird with a speckled throat and breast. It sings various lovely songs and even copies the songs of other birds. Song thrushes live in woodlands, but they also are common in gardens and city parks. They have many enemies, including birds of prey and ground predators such as cats and foxes. Squirrels, rats, and magpies often rob their nests, feasting on the eggs or chicks.

The song thrush feeds mainly on the ground, its favorite food being snails. To get at a snail, a song thrush must first break the snail's hard shell. The bird picks up the shell with its beak, then smashes the shell against a flat stone. Such stones, surrounded by many broken shells, are familiar sights in some parts of the song thrush's habitat. Sometimes a blackbird will watch a song thrush as it performs this opening ceremony. After the shell is cracked, the blackbird quickly swoops down to steal the snail before the song thrush can eat it.

The female song thrush builds a cup-shaped nest, usually in trees or bushes, using dried grasses, roots, and bits of wood. She cements these pieces together with wet mud and her saliva. Then she lines the nest with a smooth layer of mud. After she lays her eggs, the female incubates them for about two weeks. Both parents help raise the young birds.

Wood Tick
Dermacentor variabilis

Length: ⅛ inch
Method of Reproduction: egg layer
Number of Eggs: 3,000 to 6,000

Diet: blood of other animals
Home: eastern North America
Order: Ticks and mites
Family: Hard-bodied ticks

 Forests and Mountains

 Arthropods

© R. J. ERWIN / PHOTO RESEARCHERS

The wood tick is an arachnid, one of a group of animals that includes spiders, scorpions, and mites. Given its small size and its drab coloration, the wood tick would seem to be a most unremarkable creature. What makes the wood tick notable, however, is its eating habits: the wood tick feeds on the blood of humans and other animals. The life cycle of the wood tick begins when a female lays thousands of eggs in a meadow or forest. The newly hatched wood tick clings to grass or some other plant. When a suitable host (a person or an animal) passes by, the tick attaches itself to it. The tick uses its mouth to burrow through the skin of its host and suck out blood, often tripling its size before drinking its fill. Only then does the tick drop off the host. If not yet mature, the tick molts (sheds its outer skin) and finds a new host. Such repeated episodes of bloodsucking allow the tick to transfer diseases from one animal to another.

The wood tick can survive years without finding a host (and therefore without eating). The adult wood tick has few natural enemies. As a carrier of disease, the wood tick represents a real danger to hikers and others in woods and fields. It is therefore important to wear long pants and long sleeves in areas where wood ticks live. After a hike or other such outdoor activity, you should thoroughly check your own body and that of your pet for any sign of ticks.

Elegant Crested Tinamou
Eudromia elegans

Length: 15 to 16½ inches
Weight: about 1½ pounds
Diet: seeds, berries, and insects

Number of Eggs: up to 16
Home: Argentina and Chile
Order: Tinamous
Family: Tinamous

 Grasslands

 Birds

© FRANCIS GOHIER / PHOTO RESEARCHERS

Tinamous are plump, pheasantlike birds that live on the grasslands, or "pampas," of South America. The elegant crested tinamou is named for its delicate plume of long black head feathers that curve forward at the tip. Adult cocks and hens look alike. Their body plumage is dotted with white and buff-colored spots, and there is a broad white stripe above and below each dark brown eye. Young elegant crested tinamous resemble their parents, except that their crest is brown rather than black.

Elegant crested tinamous fly only awkwardly. They can run well on flat ground, but they cannot outrun predators such as wild cats and dogs. So the tinamou's best defense is to hide. Fortunately, the bird's spotted plumage is excellent camouflage on South America's open pampas.

The tinamou's eggs are vividly colored. Some people believe that they are among the most beautiful in the bird world. Like fine porcelain, the eggshells appear to have been glazed and polished.

There are 10 races, or subspecies, of elegant crested tinamou. Each looks somewhat different and lives in a slightly different habitat. Those found on the dry pampas of western Argentina are pale in color. Tinamous living in the lush, moist woodlands of northwestern Argentina are darker, with large spots.

African Clawed Toad
Xenopus laevis

Length: 5 inches (female); 2½ inches (male)
Diet: worms, insects, and other small animals
Number of Eggs: 10,000 or more each year

Home: Africa south of the Sahara
Order: Frogs and toads
Family: Water frogs

 Fresh Water

 Amphibians

© ZIG LESZCZYNSKI / ANIMALS ANIMALS / EARTH SCENES

The African clawed toad seldom leaves the water. It has adapted so well to its aquatic life-style that it can swim as well as any fish and can even swim backward! This amphibian's streamlined, scale-covered body has smooth skin, strong muscular legs and webbed toes. Curved black claws on the ends of its toes are used to stir up mud—to find food and to create clouds that help hide the clawed toad from crocodiles and other animals that prey upon it. The clawed toad can change color to match its surroundings, an ability that helps "hide" the toad from its enemies.

Instead of a tongue, the creature uses its front feet to push food toward its mouth. Sometimes it uses its toes like fingers to pick up a worm or other morsel and carry the food to its mouth. Clawed toads have big appetites. They eat almost any kind of animal they can catch—even their own tadpoles. A female clawed toad lays 10,000 or more eggs a year. These hatch into translucent tadpoles.

In summer a clawed toad's home river often dries up, forcing the creature to go overland to find another body of water. But it is more likely to burrow into the damp soil on the river bottom and enter a state called estivation, during which all the body processes slow down, and the toad uses very little energy. When rains come, the toad becomes active again.

British Toad
Bufo calamita

Length: 2 to 4 inches
Diet: insects
Home: coasts of Great Britain and Western Europe

Number of Eggs: about 5,000
Order: Tailless amphibians
Family: True toads

 Oceans and Shores

 Amphibians

© INGO ARNDT / NATURE PICTURE LIBRARY

Compared with frogs, toads are poor jumpers, and the British toad is probably the worst. This toad's limbs are so short that it can't even manage a good hop. Surprisingly, the squat British toad is quite agile. It can scurry along on its tiptoes much like a mouse.

When cornered, the British toad often tries to bluff its way out of trouble. It inflates its body, lowers its head, and stretches high on its hind legs. Then it springs forward to butt like a billy goat. Sometimes this aggressive move is enough to scare away a predator. The British toad, like all true toads, also secretes a nasty-tasting chemical from glands behind its eyes. This mild poison discourages most hungry mammals and birds. But the British toad is still eaten by turtles, snakes, frogs, and toads.

A British toad lays its eggs in shallow pools, such as the puddles that form behind sand dunes near the beach. The toad's eggs and tadpoles are specially adapted to tolerate a little salt water. Still, life in a shallow pool is risky business. The water might evaporate before the fishlike tadpoles have had time to grow into air-breathing toads. The advantage is that shallow water is easily warmed by the sun. In warm water, tadpoles mature into frogs very quickly. More importantly, by choosing shallow water, the British toad avoids competing with its close cousin, the common toad, which prefers deep ponds and lakes.

Couch's Spadefoot Toad
Scaphiopus couchi

Length: 2 to 3½ inches
Diet: insects, worms, and other invertebrates
Method of Reproduction: egg layer

Home: southwestern United States and northern Mexico
Order: Frogs and toads
Family: Spadefoot toads

 Fresh Water

 Amphibians

© JOE MCDONALD / CORBIS

Couch's spadefoot can certainly be described as "cute." Its body is small and round like an egg, and its protruding eyes are large and babyish. Although this toad's skin is covered with many wartlike bumps, it is silky smooth to the touch. Couch's spadefoot is greenish yellow across the back, and its belly is creamy white.

This toad lives on the short-grass prairie of the extreme southwestern United States and northern Mexico. It is also found in areas where mesquite and creosote bushes grow abundantly. It avoids the drying daytime heat by remaining buried in the soil or in the abandoned burrow of a small animal, such as a mouse or chipmunk. Like other spadefoot toads, this species is an efficient digger, using the long, curved spade located on each hind foot.

Couch's spadefoot toads are heard more often than they are seen. On dark, rainy nights, their choruses sound like the bleating of lambs. The noise is surprisingly loud, coming from such small creatures. After a strong rain, the frogs breed, and the females lay their eggs in large puddles. If the weather is warm, the eggs develop rapidly, hatching into tadpoles in just three days. The tadpoles must also grow quickly— before their temporary pools dry up. They can transform into adult toads in as little as two weeks. Adult spadefoots usually breed several times between April and September.

Eastern Spadefoot Toad
Scaphiopus holbrooki

Length: 1¾ to 3¼ inches
Diet: insects, spiders, and earthworms
Method of Reproduction: egg layer

Home: eastern United States, Texas, and Mexico
Order: Frogs and toads
Family: Spadefoot toads

 Cities, Towns, and Farms

 Amphibians

© DOUG WECHSLER / ANIMALS ANIMALS / EARTH SCENES

Eastern spadefoots have been found in the smoldering ashes of brush fires—totally unharmed! They can escape fire, as well as all types of enemies, by rapidly burrowing into the ground. All species of spadefoot toads have a special digging tool on the inside of their hind legs. It is shaped like a little horn, or spade. Spadefoots don't dig just to escape danger. Each morning the toads spade out a fresh burrow, where they sleep through the day. On damp summer nights, the eastern spadefoot often sits in the opening of its burrow and croaks.

When spring and summer rains form temporary water pools, eastern spadefoots quickly jump in. There the male spadefoot grabs at anything that moves. If he finds a female, he clasps her tightly around the waist. In response the female lays several long strings of gooey eggs, which her mate then fertilizes.

Two days later the eggs hatch. The emerging tadpoles must grow quickly, since their little rainpool may dry up at any time. In arid areas, such as eastern Texas and Mexico, young spadefoots can mature into adults in as little as two weeks. In this brief time, they transform from swimming, water-breathing tadpoles to hopping, air-breathing toads. Spadefoots in wetter regions, such as the Northeast, take longer to grow up. They may spend two months as tadpoles before jumping onto dry land.

Giant Toad
Bufo marinus

Length: up to 9 inches
Home: southern Texas through
  Central America to tropical
  South America; widely
  introduced elsewhere

Diet: insects
Method of Reproduction: egg
  layer
Order: Frogs and toads
Family: True toads

 Cities, Towns, and Farms

 Amphibians

© JOE MCDONALD / CORBIS

During the day, the giant toad hides under stones, or it burrows into soft soil. It comes out at night to hunt for cockroaches, beetles, and other insects. The giant toad is a native of South America, where it is very common. People have introduced the species into many new habitats, particularly to Hawaii, Puerto Rico, the Solomon Islands, and other places where sugar is raised. The toad has a big appetite and can devour vast quantities of sugar beetles, which would otherwise destroy a large part of the sugar crop. However, introducing giant toads into new places has a negative side too. The toads are now a threat to native species of frogs and toads.

When a giant toad feels threatened, glands in its shoulder ooze a milky secretion. This secretion is very poisonous. Even in small amounts, it can kill animals that attack the toad. For example, a dog that grabs a giant toad in its mouth is likely to die. The toad can squirt its poison over a distance of a foot or more. If the poison gets into the eyes of a dog or other attacker, it may cause blindness.

During the mating season, giant toads gather in ponds. The males sing a slow, low-pitched trill to attract females. After mating, a female lays long strings of eggs. A single female may produce 35,000 eggs a year! The eggs hatch into black tadpoles that change, or metamorphose, into toads in about 45 days.

36

Malayan Narrow-Mouthed Toad
Kaloula pulchra

Length: 2 to 3¼ inches
Diet: insects and worms
Method of Reproduction: egg layer

Home: Southeast Asia
Order: Frogs and toads
Family: Narrow-mouthed toads

 Forests and Mountains

 Amphibians

© DAVID A. NORTHCOTT / CORBIS

Southeast Asian children working in the garden love to uncover this fat, round toad hiding beneath the leaves. Because of its cheerful call, the Malayan narrow-mouthed toad is a favorite animal in the cities, towns, and villages of southern Asia. This is not the most colorful of Asian frogs, but its dark, chocolate-brown stripes look bold against its milky-white belly and flanks. It is very common in well-watered gardens and parks, as well as in tropical forests and fields.

Narrow-mouthed toads can all be recognized by their tiny head and extra-plump body. The front toes are sticky and broad, and resemble suction cups. The Malayan narrow-mouthed toad is rough to the touch. It can be identified by a dirty-yellow mark on its head, right between the eyes.

During the day, this toad stays hidden beneath plants and stones. At night, it hunts insects and worms in the soft, wet soil. During the rainy season, the males crowd into puddles and pools. Their noisy calls lure female toads for miles around. When the females arrive, they secrete a thin film of very tiny eggs, which the male toads fertilize. Malayan narrow-mouthed toads leave their eggs floating across the surface of the rain puddle in which they mate. After several days the eggs hatch into fishlike tadpoles, which must quickly grow into air-breathing toads before the puddle dries up.

Malaysian Horned Toad
Megophrys monticola nasuta

Length: about 5 inches
Diet: small rodents, birds, and frogs; also invertebrates
Method of Reproduction: egg layer

Home: Thailand, Malaysia, Indonesia, Borneo, and the Philippines
Order: Frogs and toads
Family: Spadefoot toads

 Rain forests

 Amphibians

© TOM MCHUGH / PHOTO RESEARCHERS

The Malaysian horned toad is one of the most bizarre-looking animals in the Asian rain forest. The skin on the toad's head protrudes beyond its nose and above its eyes, forming three soft "horns." From above, the toad looks like a pointed leaf. Its coloring perfects the disguise—like a fallen leaf, the creature is tan or chocolate brown.

True to its costume, the horned toad lives on the forest floor among piles of dead leaves. Half buried, it lies motionless, waiting for an unsuspecting prey animal to pass by. The toad's soft horns are especially sensitive to sound and probably help it sense approaching prey. This species has the ability to kill animals surprisingly larger than itself, including rodents and other frogs.

The breeding call of the Malaysian horned toad is a strange, bell-like "ching!" that rings out explosively in the night. After mating, the female lays her eggs in a rapidly flowing stream. From the eggs hatch immature tadpoles that are almost as bizarre-looking as their parents. Each tadpole hangs from the surface of the water by a broad, funnel-shaped mouth that acts like a little float. The funnel opens above the water's surface, so insects and other floating food pour into it. If the water current is strong, the tadpole can use its mouth like a suction cup to attach itself to a rock. In this way, it avoids being swept downstream.

Midwife Toad
Alytes obstetricans

Length: 1¼ to 2 inches
Diet: worms and insect larvae
Home: central and southern Europe

Number of Eggs: 30 to 40
Order: Frogs and toads
Family: Disk-tongued toads

 Fresh Water

 Amphibians

AGE FOTOSTOCK / SUPERSTOCK

The shy midwife toad lives in holes in the ground, under rocks, or in cracks in crumbling garden walls. It comes out at night to hunt for food. Midwife toads live in nearly every habitat of central and southern Europe, from near sea level to high in the mountains. In mountain areas where the ground is frozen during the winter, the toads hibernate.

Midwife toads are famous for their unusual egg-laying behavior. At night during the breeding season, the male toads gather on land and call to the females. When a female finds a male, they mate, and the female lays two long strings of eggs. The strings may contain up to 60 rather large eggs. Then the male takes over. First, he fertilizes the eggs. Then he places his back legs among the eggs, so that the eggs become wrapped around his legs. For three weeks or more, the male carries the tangled strings of eggs, attached to his legs, wherever he goes. At night, he dampens the eggs in dew, to keep them moist. When the larvae, or tadpoles, are ready to hatch, the male instinctively goes to a nearby pond or stream. He dips his hind legs into the water, and the tadpoles swim away. The tadpoles remain in the water for at least a year before they change, or metamorphose, into adults. Meanwhile, the father toad begins calling again and may soon have another mate. But because of his efforts, his offspring were well protected during the early stages of their lives.

Red-Bellied Toad
Bombina bombina

Length: 1½ to 2 inches
Diet: insects and invertebrates
Method of Reproduction: egg layer

Home: Europe
Order: Frogs and toads
Family: Discoglossid toads

 Fresh Water

 Amphibians

© STEPHEN DALTON / ANIMALS ANIMALS / EARTH SCENES

The red-bellied toad looks unremarkable, with a drab gray or green back covered with flat warts. But when frightened, this toad displays its bright red belly, a warning sign to predators not to bite. The toad's skin produces a frothy poison that stings its enemy's mouth, eyes, and nose. When extremely disturbed the red-bellied toad covers its entire body with a layer of foam. Any predator foolish enough to bite is sure to spit out this painful mouthful.

Redbellies belong to a family of toads found only in Europe, Africa, and Asia. The creatures in this family, called "discoglossids," have a short, disk-shaped tongue that is anchored firmly in their mouth. Red-bellied toads share part of their home range with the yellow-bellied toad, *Bombina variegata*. Occasionally the two species interbreed and produce orange-bellied offspring.

The redbelly spends its entire life in water. Between April and August, males call loudly to attract mates. When a female comes within reach, the male grabs her around the waist. As he fertilizes her eggs, she deposits them in small clumps on underwater plants. The eggs hatch into fishlike tadpoles, which turn into toads when they are about ¾ of an inch long. The young are ready to mate in about two years. Some red-bellied toads live to be over 12 years old.

Seychelles Tortoise
Testudo gigantea

Length: up to 4½ feet
Weight: up to 500 pounds
Diet: plants
Method of Reproduction: egg
  layer

Home: Aldabra in the
  Seychelles Islands
Order: Turtles and tortoises
Family: Tortoises

  Grasslands

Reptiles

© WOLFGANG KAEHLER / CORBIS

The Seychelles tortoise is the only survivor of a group of giant tortoises that once lived on islands all across the Indian Ocean. Today this species survives in the wild only on a ring of four coral islands called Aldabra. Aldabra is part of the Seychelles Islands off the east coast of Africa. Fortunately, as many as 150,000 of the tortoises can be found there today.

The people of the islands realize that their native giants are valuable tourist attractions, and they protect them. People have also transported captive Seychelles tortoises to the Mauritius and Réunion islands, off the east coast of Madagascar.

Besides the Seychelles tortoise, the only other giant tortoise in the world is its cousin on the Galápagos Islands, half a world away near Ecuador. Both the Galápagos tortoise and the Seychelles tortoise have an enormous, domed shell, or carapace. Most Seychelles tortoises sport a shiny, dark-brown carapace. The carapace is made of many fused plates that are marked with circular grooves. The tortoise's shell has a special protective plate, called a nuchal scute, over the back of the neck. Like most tortoises, this species retreats into its shell when frightened. Although the tortoise's short tail cannot be withdrawn, it ends in a horny claw, which discourages attack. The animal's powerful legs are covered with hard scales that protect its skin from the drying heat and salty sea air.

Yellow-legged Tortoise
Testudo carbonaria

Diet: fruits and other plant matter
Method of Reproduction: egg layer

Length: up to 20 inches
Home: South America
Order: Turtles and tortoises
Family: Tortoises

 Rain forests

 Reptiles

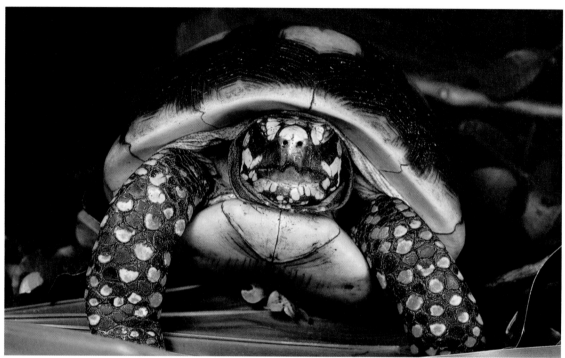

© STEPHEN COOPER / PHOTO RESEARCHERS

The yellow-legged tortoise lives on land in moist tropical rain forests. It travels about during the day and on moonlit nights, looking for fruits and other soft plant food. The tortoise has no teeth, so it cannot eat tough stems and other fibrous plant parts. Instead, it uses the hard, sharp edges of its jaws to crush soft food and chop it into pieces small enough to swallow.

The tortoise's only defense is its shell. But the shell can be a hindrance, too. As the creature moves around on its short, stumpy legs, its boxlike shell adds weight and slows down the tortoise's progress.

When a predator approaches, the yellow-legged tortoise simply withdraws into the safety of its shell. The top of the shell, or carapace, is fused to the vertebrae that make up the tortoise's backbone. The carapace consists of many horny plates called scutes. The scutes are arranged in a definite pattern that is different from tortoise to tortoise. Like a human fingerprint, the scutes help people identify individual tortoises.

Soon after mating takes place, the female digs a hole in the ground. There she deposits her eggs and gently covers them with soil. Her work complete, she leaves the eggs, never to return again. The warmth of the sun incubates the eggs. The baby tortoises are born with a soft shell and must fend for themselves immediately.

Clown Triggerfish
Balistoides conspicillum

Length: up to 15 inches
Diet : sea urchins, coral
  polyps, mollusks, crabs, and
  tube worms
Method of Reproduction: egg
  layer

Home: tropical Indo-Pacific
  oceans
Order: Puffers
Family: Triggerfishes and
  filefishes

 Oceans and Shores

Fish

© TOM BRAKEFIELD / CORBIS

With its wild and colorful markings, the clown triggerfish is a much-sought-after marine-aquarium fish. But beware! This "pet" has strong, sharp teeth and will bite anything within reach. It is not recommended for beginner aquarists or for community tanks, because it may attack other fish. In the wild, this species lives near coral reefs and tropical lagoons.

Clown triggerfish occur in a variety of colors. All have bright white spots on the head and body, and a clownish smear of color around the mouth. The mouth is full of sharp teeth, with an outer row of long fangs and an inner row of short spikes.

Triggerfish are named for two unique spines located in the dorsal fin (atop the back). The front spine is very long and strong. Behind it is a smaller spine that acts like a "trigger" mechanism to lock both spines in an upright position. When a triggerfish is frightened, it darts into a narrow crevice or tiny hole. It then erects its spines to wedge itself tightly in place. If it has the chance, the fish prefers to back into its escape hole, so it can use its sharp teeth to defend itself.

When the female spawns, she lays a mass of gluey eggs in a shallow pit in the sand and gravel. She or her mate guard the nest fiercely, even attacking divers who venture close. Guard duty does not last long, because the eggs hatch within 24 hours.

Albacore Tuna
Thunnus alalunga

Length: up to 5 feet
Weight: up to 90 pounds
Diet: small fish, squid, and crustaceans
Method of Reproduction: egg layer

Home: North Atlantic and North Pacific oceans and Mediterranean Sea
Order: Perchlike fishes
Family: Mackerels

 Oceans and Shores

 Fish

© RICHARD HERMANN / VISUALS UNLIMITED

The albacore tuna is one of the ocean's most valuable fish. You can find its meat at your grocery store in cans labeled "white-meat tuna." Unfortunately, this fish's meat may be too popular. Overhunting has reduced albacore populations around the world. Though they are not in danger of extinction, these fish are now much harder to find than they once were.

Albacore love to swim in the clear blue water in the middle of the ocean, but they do not often find enough food there. As strange as it may sound, the deep water of the open sea is much like a desert. The soil and nutrients that wash from the land into the coastal waters don't reach this far into the sea. So few plants grow there. With few plants to eat, there are even fewer "herbivores," animals that eat plants. So meat-eating animals such as the albacore must travel far and wide to find enough small fish and crustaceans to eat. Albacore in the Pacific Ocean, for example, swim north along the entire coast of North America, following schools of squid and other small fish.

Summer is also the time for laying eggs. But where does a fish make a nest in the middle of an ocean? The ocean floor is too deep. So the female albacore releases large numbers of eggs into the water, where they float like so many bubbles. When they hatch, the young fish are on their own.

47